WITHDRAWN

# Child Slavery in Modern Times

# Child Slavery in Modern Times

**Shirlee P. Newman**

**Franklin Watts**
A Division of Grolier Publishing
New York • London • Hong Kong • Sydney
Danbury, Connecticut

*For children everywhere.*
*May they all be as free as our beloved Abby, David, Todd, and Haley.*

**Note to readers:** Definitions for words in **bold** can be found in the Glossary at the back of this book.

Photographs ©: AP/Wide World Photos: 33 (Mike Albans), 20 (Jean-Marc Bouju), 51 (K. M. Choudary), 25 (Kent Gilbert), 44 (Amy Sancetta), 16 (Stephan Savoia), 34 (Kathy Willens), 22; Corbis Sygma: 5 bottom, 36 (Bob Daemmrich), 18 (Robert Grossman), 2, 11 (J. P. Laffont), 19 (David Ga); Corbis-Bettmann: 40 (Richard Hamilton), 30 (UPI); Denver Post: 21 (Dave Buresh); Impact Visuals: 46 (Donna DeCesare), 5 top, 31 (Lina Pallotta); Liaison Agency, Inc.: 6 (Bourg), 38 (Nancy Buirski), 14, 15 (Tony Comiti), 9 (Daniels), 41 (Bill Gillette), 42 (Paul S. Howell), 49 (Robert Nickelsberg); National Geographic Image Collection: 26 (Stephanie Maze), 13 (James Stanfield); The Image Works: 8 (Bob Strong); University of Maryland, Baltimore: 28 (Albin O. Kuhn Library & Gallery).

Cover illustration by Carol Werner.

Visit Franklin Watts on the Internet at:
http://publishing.grolier.com

**Library of Congress Cataloging-in-Publication Data**

Newman, Shirlee Petkin.
    Child slavery in modern times / by Shirlee P. Newman
        p.      cm.— (Watts Library)
    Includes bibliographical references and index.
    Summary: Discusses cases where children are forced to work against their wills in difficult and dangerous conditions in various countries around the world.
    ISBN 0-531-11696-4 (lib. bdg.)    0-531-16540-X (pbk.)
    1. Child slaves—Juvenile literature. 2. Slavery—Juvenile literature. [1. Child abuse. 2. Child labor. 3. Slavery.] I. Title. II. Series.
HT871 .N48 2000
306.3'62'083—dc21                                               00-038199

# Contents

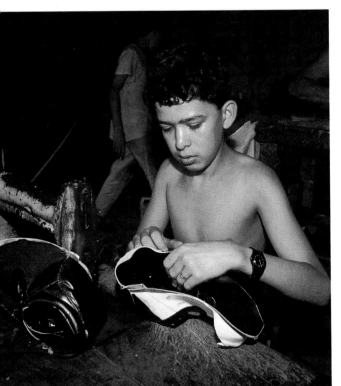

*After being freed from a carpet factory, Iqbal Masih dedicated the rest of his life to helping other children.*

# Chapter One

# Child Slavery Today

Ten-year-old Iqbal Masih lived in Pakistan, a poor country in Asia. When he was four years old, Iqbal went to work in a hot, dusty carpet factory to pay back money his father had borrowed from the factory's owner. Iqbal could never pay it back. The owner charged him for his daily bowl of rice and fined him whenever he fell asleep because the work was so boring. He'd have to work at the factory for the rest of his life, he thought. Iqbal went to the police and told them

*Like Iqbal, this girl works long hours at a loom in a carpet factory in Pakistan.*

how badly he was treated. The police listened to what he said, and then took him back to the factory. The owner beat him and chained him to the **loom**, the frame used to weave carpets.

Iqbal went to see a human-rights group who thought it was wrong to make children work. With their help, he was freed from the factory and enrolled in their school. He learned to read, write, and speak so well that he was able to lead other children in public protests against child labor. Newspapers in several countries wrote stories about him and in 1994, he was invited to speak in Sweden and the United States.

For his efforts to end child slavery, Iqbal won the Reebok Youth in Action Award in December 1994. He planned to use the prize money for law school. He wanted to become a lawyer, so he could help to free other children, but he never got the chance. In 1995, Iqbal was shot and killed in Pakistan while he was riding his bicycle. Most people blame the carpet manufacturers for his murder because they lost business as a result of Iqbal's work. In 2000, the Sweden-based organization, Children's World, named Iqbal the winner of the first Children's Prize for Outstanding Children.

*In Calcutta, children face the hazards of recycling batteries.*

## What Is Child Slavery?

The United Nations, often called the UN, is a group of nations working for peace and the good of **humanity**, or all people. In 1948, the UN's Declaration of Human Rights said that slavery and the slave trade (buying and selling human beings) should be banned. The UN also said that the word *slave* describes anyone who can't stop working or change jobs. It also describes someone who works to pay off debts. Children who are separated from their families, forced to work at dangerous jobs, or perform tasks too hard for their age may also be called slaves.

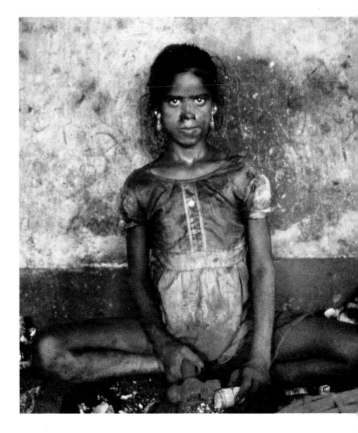

9

In 1989, the UN tried to improve children's lives by creating another document. This declaration said that children everywhere must be protected from abuse, torture, harmful punishments, and **exploitation**. However, employers in countries that voted for the document continue to hire children. They do this for two reasons. First, employers pay children less than adults for the same work. Second, children are usually afraid to complain about bad working conditions. Anti-Slavery International, an organization that works to eliminate slavery, says as many as 200 million children in the world may be working when they should be in school.

## Debt Bondage

The word **bondage** comes from the word bound, meaning "tied." Children like Iqbal Masih, who work to pay back their family's debt, are in **debt bondage**. In 1995, a writer who visited a sporting-goods factory in Pakistan saw boys and girls as young as five years old making soccer balls that were sold in the United States and Europe. The children were forbidden to talk to one another, and the room in which they worked was kept dark so that anyone who objected to child labor would have trouble taking pictures. The children were allowed one 30-minute break each day, and punished if they fell asleep or wasted material. They were punished severely if they complained to their parents about working conditions or spoke to strangers outside the factory. Punishments included being hung upside down, starved, beaten, and whipped.

**A Mother Speaks**

"When my children were three, I told them they must be prepared to work for the good of the family," a Pakistani mother said. "I told them again and again that they would be bonded. By the time they turned five they were prepared, and they went to work for masters in far-away villages without complaining."

Many children in Asian countries work at dangerous jobs in brick factories, steel mills, and stone-crushing plants. A twelve-year-old who had been making bricks in India since he was six said, "I cannot pay back the loan, so I must work. I cannot go anywhere. I am a prisoner."

*These young children work in a brick factory.*

## Danger in the Water

Marcelo, who lives in the Philippine Islands in the Pacific Ocean, started diving from a fishing boat when he was ten years old. He explained that divers swim shoulder to shoulder.

They bang a weight against **coral**, a limestone formation on the ocean floor, to scare the fish into a net. With no diving equipment the boys dive as deep as 100 feet (30.5 meters) to fasten and free the net. One year three boys from Marcelo's ship drowned.

Boys who work on fishing platforms off the coast of Sumatra, an Indonesian island in Southeast Asia have also drowned. For several months, 1,500 wooden fishing platforms, are "home" to thousands of boys. They haul up fishnets from six in the morning till midnight. In the busiest season, which lasts for three months, they start work at 1:00 A.M. and work around the clock. They take short naps during occasional breaks—that is the only time they sleep.  Some of the boys have fallen from the platforms and drowned. Others have drowned when the rickety wooden platforms fell apart in stormy weather.

# Camel Jockeys

**Traffickers** or slave traders take four- and five-year-old boys from several Asian countries to the Arabian Peninsula, where gamblers bet on camel races. The boys are given very little food so that they won't gain weight, and are forced to race camels until they're eleven or twelve. Although they are tied to the camels' backs, some boys fall off and are injured or killed. Those who become crippled are sent out to beg.

Juru Miah, a four-year-old boy from Bangladesh, was found in the desert after surviving five days without food or

water. He had been brought to the United Arab Emirates to work as a camel jockey. From his hospital bed, Juru said: "They used to give me rice for lunch and bread for dinner, nothing else. Most of the time I wasn't allowed to eat or drink. I felt hungry and thirsty all the time. Racketeers forced me to ride camels." Juru said that when he refused, he was thrown on the ground and beaten. He was left alone to die in the desert because he was considered a "bad investment."

*Children serve as jockeys in camel races on the coast of Oman.*

13

# Child Slavery in Latin America

Thousands of children work in gold mines in Peru, South America. In the 1990s, when the government began to investigate, the children were moved into the jungle. They were kept in camps located a week's journey from the nearest town so they couldn't be found. A thirteen-year-old girl whose father sent her to work as a cook in a jungle mining camp said she expected the same man who brought her there to come and take her home. She hasn't heard from him since she arrived. A landowner in the area said that she would never go home.

In countries in Central America, South America, and the West Indies, young boys are taken to plantations, locked in armed camps, and forced to dig ditches, cut sugarcane, work in mines underground, or do whatever else their slave masters demand. In the Dominican Republic, a country in the West Indies, a Dutch woman told a teenage girl that she could get a scholarship in the Netherlands and study while she did light housework for the woman. "When we arrived there [the Netherlands] she suddenly seemed like a differ-

ent person," the girl said. The woman forced her to get a passport using a false name and age. Then the woman said the girl owed her so much money for transportation that she had to get a high-paying job to earn enough to pay it back. Forced to work, the girl never had a chance to learn.

*These children work in mines in Colombia.*

*Moctar Teyeb lived as a slave for nineteen years in Mauritania, a country in western Africa.*

# Chapter Two

# Children as Property

"I am a runaway slave," Moctar Teyeb said when he spoke at a school in Dover, Massachusetts, in 1999. He was born into a life of slavery in a village in Mauritania, a country in western Africa. "According to Mauritanian tradition and local law, I am still my master's property because I do not have a warrant from him to prove my freedom," he explained. "We were **chattels**—bought, sold, and bred like farm animals."

Most slave owners in Mauritania are Muslim Arabs—people who speak Arabic and follow the faith of **Islam**. In the past, the word *Arabs* meant "**nomads**," people who moved from place to place with their animals. Now the word is used to describe most people in northern Africa, and some people in other countries, including the United States. Some Arabs have dark skin, others have light skin. Blacks are a large minority group in Mauritania, and Moctar Teyeb is a black Muslim. He became a slave because his parents were slaves, even though the Islam religion forbids Muslims from enslaving one another. As a boy, Moctar hauled water from a well, herded cattle, and took care of his master's camels and children. "My only reason for [living] was to care for my master's family's every need," he said. He escaped at nineteen when he was sent to the city to do an errand.

Slavery has been declared illegal in Mauritania several times, but the law is not enforced, and the government does nothing to help freed slaves begin lives on their own. Arab slave traders still break up slave families by selling children away from their parents and separating husbands and wives and brothers and sisters, just as they did centuries ago.

**Priests' Slaves**

In parts of Ghana, another West African country, a girl may become a tribal priest's slave if someone in her family commits any sort of crime.

# Slavery in Sudan

Most people in northern Sudan, the largest country in Africa, are Muslim Arabs. People in southern Sudan speak their own language and are either Christian or have their own particular tribal religion.

In April 1999, Arab **mercenaries** from North Sudan rode into the south. (Mercenaries are soldiers who will fight for any country that pays them.) They killed cattle, destroyed crops, burned homes, poisoned wells, and took four hundred Dinka men, women, and children as slaves. For many years, northern and southern Sudan have been fighting a religious war. Thousands of southern Sudanese have been kidnapped and shipped in railroad cars to slave markets in the north. Some of the slaves' new masters force them to become Muslims.

*Thousands of Dinka people have been captured and enslaved.*

*A member of a human-rights group pays a slave trader money to free slaves in Sudan.*

In 1991, six-year-old Akuac Malong, her older brother, and their mother were on the way to get water. Suddenly soldiers from the north came thundering into their village on camels and horses. "I was running with Akuac for the trees when a horseman grabbed her," her mother said. "I was afraid if I chased the horseman, he would kill me." Akuac and her brother were tied to the back of a horse and taken north and sold into slavery.

"I was badly treated," Akuac said, when a human-rights group from Switzerland bought her freedom seven years later. Her master had given her only leftovers to eat. She had to wash clothes, haul water, gather firewood, and cook. He tried to force her to become Muslim and change her name to an Arabic one. She kept her own faith by praying and secretly singing Christian hymns. "And my name is my name," she said. "Nobody can change that."

## Fifth Graders Fight Slavery

When a fifth-grade class in Aurora, Colorado, heard about slavery in Sudan, the students contacted the American Anti-Slavery Group on the Internet. They learned that they could

*This fifth-grade class at an Aurora, Colorado, elementary school raised money to free slaves in Sudan.*

buy a slave's freedom for about $50 through a Swiss human-rights group. The class raised money by selling lemonade, toys, and T-shirts. News of their fund-raising drive spread, and contributions as high as $5,000 came streaming in. Before long, the class had enough money to buy freedom for a thousand slaves.

Opinions differ about what to do about slavery. Some people say buying slaves their freedom encourages slave traders to buy or kidnap more people so that they'll have more to sell. Others think civil wars must be stopped before the slavery problem can be solved. Still others think slavery would gradually die out if poverty were eliminated. The Swiss human-rights group continues to buy the freedom of Sudanese slaves, but thousands of people are still in bondage.

## Children in Wars

Thousands of children are forced to fight in wars. A 1999 news report estimated that 12,000 children have been kidnapped from northern Uganda, a country south of Sudan, and forced to work for the northern Sudanese army.

Roseline would stay with them in England as their guest. Guest? In England, Roseline worked eighteen hours a day cleaning, cooking, washing, ironing, and taking care of the couple's five children. She was paid nothing, had no time off, and slept on the floor. One day, she went to a window and asked a neighbor for something to eat. The neighbor helped Roseline escape, and she eventually returned to Nigeria.

Seba, a girl from Mali, a country in western Africa that was once a French colony, also became a domestic slave. "I was raised by my grandmother," Seba said. When Seba was six years old, a Frenchwoman asked her grandmother if she could take Seba to Paris to care for her children. The woman said that she would send Seba to school there, but she never did. Seba was a domestic slave for fourteen years. "I started work before seven in the morning and finished about eleven at night," she said. After she was beaten, locked up, and tortured, the French Committee Against Modern Slavery freed Seba and placed her in a foster home.

In Costa Rica, most household slaves come from Nicaragua, a neighboring country in Central America. Some slaves are forced into doing potentially harmful tasks. "The senora [woman] told me to get up on a ladder and wash the walls," said a teenage girl in Costa Rica. "I thought that was really dangerous, but she said if I didn't do it, I had to leave." The teenager was afraid to leave because she was an illegal **immigrant**, and she thought she'd go to jail if the police found out. She climbed the ladder and washed the walls.

## Long Hours

Domestic slaves who live in their employers' homes may be called upon to work any time during the day or night.

*Many girls from Nicaragua go to Costa Rica for a better life, but only find themselves working as domestic slaves.*

# Traffickers in Asia

Thousands of girls in China are taken from bus stops, train stations, and labor markets where they go to seek employment. A middleman promises the girls good jobs, but they end up as household slaves or are sold into abusive "marriages." Traffickers buy boys from poor parents in Cambodia, a country in Southeast Asia, and sell them in Thailand, a neighboring country. Twelve-year-old Chan Nang was taken to Bangkok, Thailand's capital. There he was sold to a woman

*After being promised good jobs, some girls end up washing dishes and scrubbing floors.*

who forced him to beg and steal on the city's busy streets and give the money to her. "Sometimes I could satisfy her," Chan Nang told the police, lifting his shirt to show them two deep scars, "but often I was beaten because I made less than 1,000 *baht* [$25] a day."

For centuries, it was legal to sell children in Japan and China. Although it is now illegal in both countries, some Chinese parents still sell their teenage daughters into marriage. When a man from a poor mountain village outside Beijing, the capital of China, couldn't find a bride in his own village, he came to Ma's village and paid her father 2,000 *yuan* (about $300) for her. "I miss my home," she whispered to a newspaper reporter. "I want my mother."

Some teenage girls in other Asian countries get married because they are talked into it, then find that the "marriage" was just a trick to get free labor. Many household slaves become chattels.

*Many children worked in the U.S. cotton mills during the Industrial Revolution in the 1800s.*

# Chapter Four

# Working in Factories

Many child slaves end up working in **sweatshops**—places where the owners do not obey laws about working conditions, how long people may work, and how much they should be paid. Sweatshops in the United States sprang up in the 1800s during the Industrial Revolution. Many factory owners needed more workspace and more workers, so they hired smaller companies to do some of their work. The small firms quickly set up makeshift workplaces.

In the early 1900s, after 146 young European immigrants, including many teenagers, were killed in a sweatshop fire in New York City, several states passed laws against sweatshops. By the 1940s, most of the sweatshops were out of business. Since the late 1970s, however, the number of sweatshops in the United States has increased because so many immigrants

*This photo shows the damage done by fire at Triangle Shirtwaist Fire in 1911.*

have come to the United States. Many of these people don't speak English and know nothing about U.S. labor laws. As a result, sweatshop owners can exploit them. Almost every city in which immigrants have settled has its sweatshops.

In 1990, more than 50,000 people, some of them children, worked in 4,500 sweatshops in New York State alone. Most New York sweatshops serve the clothing industry.

*This nine-year-old boy works in a clothing factory in Brooklyn, New York.*

## Home Sweatshops

Some children work at home. A Vietnamese woman who investigated sweatshop conditions in her community in New York, reported that one boy and three girls were working together in a small apartment. One of the children was making bows on an old sewing machine in the corner. A smaller girl cut off extra ribbon. The next one glued them with a glue gun, and the boy put them into hair clips.

Their mother explained that the children started work as soon as they came home from school. The work had to be ready by pickup time the next day, and they often had to stay up most of the night to finish it. The mother said the children were usually so tired that they couldn't keep up with other students in class, but she had no choice. Her children had to help out. She went to English classes in the morning. Until she learned to speak English, she couldn't find a job that would support them.

## Chinese Immigrants

Ships carrying Chinese people come to the United States every year. In 1993, a ship with 286 young Chinese men aboard ran aground off New York's Long Island. The passengers, who had borrowed thousands of dollars to pay for the trip and had been on the crowded ship for four months. Most of them jumped into the water, hoping to escape. The U.S. Coast Guard rescued some of them, but ten people drowned.

Those who survived said they had come to America hoping to earn enough money to pay for their passage and find a better life. They said if they went back to China without paying their debt, they'd probably be killed. Teenagers have been found in packing cases on other ships, and in 1999, when 132 illegal Chinese immigrants landed in Savannah, Georgia, a government spokesman said 51 of them were teenagers.

## Snakeheads

People who smuggle Chinese immigrants into the United States are sometimes called snakeheads.

*These Chinese immigrants from the ship that ran aground on Long Island hoped to live and work in the United States.*

*This boy makes sneakers in a sweatshop in Honduras.*

## Promises, Promises

Urged by college students, human-rights groups, and the U.S. government, many large U.S. clothing companies made some promises about how they were going to change the way they treated their factory workers in 1997. They said that they would set basic labor standards in their factories in Latin America, the Caribbean, and Asia, and that the factories there would be open for inspection. The students later learned that the companies had hired their own "inspectors." The students insisted that local human-rights groups whom they trusted, do the inspecting.

Pacific Ocean. More than 50,000 people from China, the Philippines, Bangladesh, and Thailand, came to Saipan after receiving promises of a good job in the United States. Instead, they found themselves working seven days a week in sweat-shops. In Saipan, teenagers have been forced to work up to twelve hours a day and threatened with beatings if they refused. Their passports were taken away and they were not allowed to leave the factory grounds.

*Children often work
in the fields alongside
their parents all
day long.*

# Chapter Five

# Working in the Fields

Many families travel hundreds, sometimes thousands of miles to pick fruit and vegetables as soon as they ripen. These families are **migrant workers**, and they often include children. **Federal** laws for children who work on farms are not as strict as the laws for children in other kinds of work. Twelve- and thirteen-year-olds can do farm labor with their parents' approval, and fourteen-year-olds can work in the fields with no restrictions. On small farms, federal law does not protect child workers at all, even though farmwork is especially dangerous for children.

It is estimated that 300 children die of farm-related accidents every year, and more than 23,000 are injured. In New Jersey, in 1996, a five-year-old boy's hand was ripped off in a conveyor belt. He was helping his mother pack watermelons because day care was not available. A four-year-old was killed by a car in Oregon as he and his family crossed a dirt road to get to asparagus fields. It was so early in the morning that it was still dark. A sixteen-year-old boy was electrocuted when he was helping to build a grain bin. State governments have passed laws protecting children who work in the fields, but farmers need workers and migrant families need money, so these laws are often ignored. Children as young as four years old work in fields at least part of the day, even though they often get sick from **pesticides**—chemicals sprayed on fields to kill insects.

*Farm workers are exposed to dangerous pesticides sprayed from planes.*

## Children Pick by Hand

In recent years, giant international **corporations,** big power-ful companies called **agribusinesses**, have bought up many small farms. They now use machines to plant and harvest some crops. But children still pick many oranges, apples, berries, cherries, peaches, asparagus, cucumbers, tomatoes, lettuce and other fruits and vegetables by hand.

*This photo shows a boy harvesting vegetables.*

Jose Martinez of Lawrence, Michigan, was in second grade when he started working in the fields. The first crop he picked was blueberries. He said he was so young he didn't really understand why he and his family were out there. As he got older, he learned that it was his responsibility to work. "Until we were old enough to work legally, we'd get paid under the names of older family members," he said. "We needed the money and me and my brothers were an essential part of our family's income. We just did it."

Most migrant families travel to the fields in old **jalopies**— worn-out cars or trucks that often break down. Other

*For some migrant families, old buses double as their homes while on the road or at the fields.*

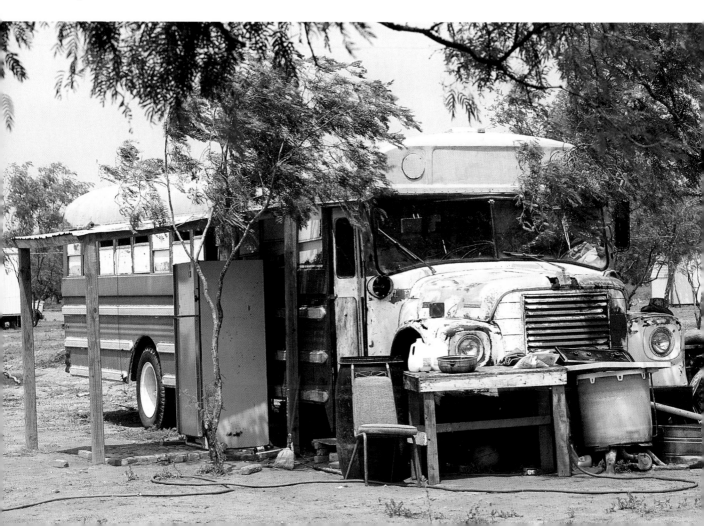

migrants travel with neighbors or friends in secondhand school buses. Teenage migrants who travel alone are called **freewheelers**. Some of them hitchhike or hop rides on freight trains.

Migrant workers from the south usually travel north to states along the Canadian border. After harvesting crops there, some head south, picking late crops and second plantings on the way home. When fruits and vegetables dry up in **droughts** or rot in floods, the families may have made the trip for nothing. Even when the families get work, some don't break even after they count up traveling expenses.

Not all migrant families travel north, and not all migrant children work in the fields every day. Some of them stay in the workers' quarters and care for younger children. One family left their home in Texas and went east to potato fields in Alabama. The nine-year-old boy in the family spent the first few days caring for his younger brothers and sisters. Their

*A teenage Mexican immigrant sits in his bunk at a migrant farm camp in Pennsylvania.*

mother picked out rotten, green, and misshapen potatoes as they bounced along a conveyor belt. Her husband loaded the others into sacks and piled them onto a trailer. At 7:00 P.M., after working for twelve hours, the children's parents came back to the workers' quarters. Portable bathrooms and one shower for the whole camp were outside. The walls were so thin that a crying baby in the next room kept the family awake all night. The following day the nine-year-old boy worked in the potato fields with his father, and his mother took care of the younger children.

## Mexican Migrants

Many migrant workers are poor people from Mexico who think they'll earn more money in the United States than they can earn in their own country. Some enter the United States without proper papers because the papers cost money and take a long time to get. Many of these migrant workers are teenagers. Some come with their parents. Others come alone.

**Coyotes**

Mexicans who smuggle people into the United States are often called coyotes.

"When I was fourteen," a Mexican boy said, "a coyote came and told us that farmers in the U.S. needed workers." The boy's father agreed to pay the coyote when the boy had crossed the border and was working. The father put up his land as **collateral,** something valuable to keep until a debt is paid. "My mother cried when I left home because she had heard that criminals along the border steal from immigrants and some even get killed. I told her I'd be careful, but she wouldn't stop crying," the boy said.

*Some Mexican migrants work in the U.S. fields, hoping to earn more money than they could back home.*

The trip was scary. Mexican police officers stopped the bus the boy was on while he was still in Mexico and said he had to get off unless he gave them some money. Luckily, the woman who sat next to him gave them some. When the bus arrived at a town in the Mexican desert, the coyote made the boy and a few others get off. They waited in the town for three days. Then they hid out on the desert until nightfall, lying flat on the ground until helicopters with bright searchlights circling overhead finally left. After walking until morning, they came to a town. "I didn't even know we had crossed the border," the boy said. "We were in the United States."

The coyote packed the teenagers into a van, drove them hundreds of miles to Washington State and left them in an empty barn. "I'll come back and take you to work," he said. He never did, but some people in a nearby church gave them food and warm clothes and found them jobs. The money the fourteen-year-old boy earned picking cherries from early morning till night was sent to his father. It was enough to pay back the coyote. The boy then bought himself the first pair of new shoes he'd ever had, and some clothes to take home to his brothers and sisters.

## Public Awareness

For decades, television programs have reported on the difficult life and poor working conditions of the migrant workers and their families. In 1960, CBS Television aired a groundbreaking program called *Harvest of Shame* on Thanksgiving Day. The program showed how badly migrant workers and their children were treated in the United States. Thousands of people wrote to their congressional representatives and asked them to pass stricter labor laws to protect children in the fields.

Thirty-eight years later, in 1998, another television program showed that children were still working in the fields. "They are working hard for low pay, struggling to help their families survive," the announcer said. A family who had traveled 5,000 miles (8,045 kilometers) in an old van that caught on fire was interviewed. The eleven-year-old boy in the family had back pain because he spent all day bent over picking cucumbers. His fifth-grade teacher was also interviewed. She said the boy was bright but reads below grade level because he misses so much school. His four-year-old sister picked berries. His ten-year-old sister packed them in boxes.

## Asian Field Workers

Although it is now illegal for landowners in Pakistan to lend people money in exchange for their labor, entire families are still becoming bonded workers. Chatan Bheel, the father of two teenage sons, borrowed $300 from the owner of the sugar plantation on which he and his sons worked. With interest, the $300 grew to $3,000 in less than a year. When Bheel complained, the landowner put Bheel and his sons in chains to keep them from trying to escape. Even though armed men guarded the fields, Chatan Bheel, with his legs in heavy iron chains, made his way through chest-high sugarcane until he came to a blacksmith, who cut him loose. "I am still not free," he said when he got to a camp for freed bonded workers. "If I leave here, I can always be caught." His sons, who were released in a government raid on the plantation, had already been recaptured.

Small Pakistani children are tied together as they plow, plant, and gather grain. "They are cheaper to run than tractors and smarter than oxen," a Pakistani landowner said. He

preferred children between seven and ten years of age "because they have the most energy."

In Sri Lanka, an island country about 20 miles (32 km) off the southeast coast of India, children pick tea leaves and place them in heavy baskets strapped to their backs. Some children in Sri Lanka have died because they swallowed small amounts

*Many Pakistani children have to work to pay off their families' debts.*

of poisonous pesticides—on purpose. They were trying to get sick so they could take time off.

## Rescued

In December 1999, slave traffickers took seventy-one children from Mali to Ivory Coast, a neighboring country in Africa, and forced them to work long hours on a cotton plantation without pay. The children were rescued and returned to Mali, where a privately run school is helping them adjust to life in freedom. There the children, who are between the ages of seven and fifteen, learn to read and write.

The school also arranges for them to become **apprentices** to local handicraft workers, blacksmiths, and other tradespeople. Some of the children also learn how to raise chickens and herd animals so they can decide whether they'd rather work in a large town or a small country village. A few of the children left the school and returned to Ivory Coast. The children thought they could earn a great deal of money there, now that they were rid of the traffickers.

## How You Can Help

Look for the growers' names on fruit and vegetable cartons at the supermarket. Go to the library and ask a librarian to help you find their addresses. Write or e-mail them, asking if children work in their fields. Write to your U.S. congressional representatives and tell them we need new laws protecting children who work in agriculture.

Contact one of the antislavery or human-rights groups listed on the following pages by mail or through the Internet and ask them to send you up-to-date information. Write letters or send e-mails to the heads of countries that permit any form of child slavery.

*These children participated in the Global March Against Child Labor in Pakistan in 1998.*

# Glossary

**agribusiness**—a big company or corporation that grows and packs fruits and vegetables

**apprentice**—a person who works for a period of time in a craft or trade in return for instruction

**baht**—Thai money

**bondage**—slavery, captivity

**chattel**—a person who is treated as if he or she were a thing; a slave

**collateral**—something valuable given in place of a debt until the debt is paid

**coral**—a limestone formation in the ocean floor

**corporation**—a big company

**debt bondage**—working to pay back a debt

**domestic**—household

**drought**—a long period without rain

**exploitation**—being taken advantage of, usually by being underpaid

**federal**—U.S. government

**freewheeler**—a migrant worker who travels alone

**humanity**—all the people of the world

**immigrant**—a person who comes to live in another country

**Islam**—the religion followed by Muslims

**jalopy**—an old, worn-out car or truck

**loom**—the frame on which a carpet is made

**mercenary**—a soldier who is paid to fight for a foreign country

**migrant worker**—a person who leaves home to find work

**nomad**—a person who moves from place to place

**pesticide**—a chemical sprayed on crops to kill insects

**sweatshop**—a workplace where labor laws are not obeyed

**trafficker**—a slave trader; a person who kidnaps, buys children or tricks them into traveling long distances, and then sells them to others.

**yuan**—Chinese money

# To Find Out More

## Books

Ennew, Judith. *Exploitation of Children.* Austin, Texas: Steck-Vaughn, 1997.

Freedman, Russell. *Kids at Work, Lewis Hine and the Crusade Against Child Labor.* New York: Clarion, 1994.

Greene, Laura. *Child Labor: Then and Now.* New York: Franklin Watts, 1992.

Meltzer, Milton. *Cheap Raw Material, How Our Youngest Workers Are Exploited and Abused.* New York: Viking, 1994.

Springer, Jane. *Listen to Us, the World's Working Children.* Toronto: Groundwood Books, 1997.

Stanley, Jerry. *Children of the Dust Bowl: The True Story of the School at Weedpatch Camp*, New York: Crown, 1992.

Steele, Philip. *The Children's Atlas of the World*. Danbury, CT: Franklin Watts, 2000.

Weiner, Sandra. *Small Hands, Big Hands. Seven Stories of Mexican-American Migrant Workers and their Families*. New York: Pantheon, 1970.

# Organizations and Online Sites

American Anti-Slavery Group
198 Tremont Street, #421
Boston, MA 02116
*http://www.anti-slavery.org*
This organization is dedicated to abolishing slavery around the world.

Anti-Slavery International
Thomas Clarkson House
The Stableyard
Broomgrove Road
London, England, SW9 9TL
*http://www.antislavery.org*
This organization fights slavery, child labor, and forced marriage.

Free the Children International
1750 Steeles Ave. W., Suite 218
Concord, Ontario, Canada L4K 2L7
*http://www.freethechildren.org/*
This organization works to free children from exploitation, abuse, and poverty.

Save the Children
*http://www.savethechildren.org*
This organization helps children in need around the world, and its website provides information on how you can help too.

UNICEF
3 UN Plaza
New York, NY 10017
*http://www.unicef.org/*
This organization supports children's rights and works to protect and improve children's lives worldwide.

U. S. House of Representatives
Washington, DC 20515
*http://www.house.gov*
From this website, you can find your local representative.

U. S. Senate
Washington, DC 20510
*http://www.senate.gov*
At the Senate website, you can locate the senator for your area.

The White House
l600 Pennsylvania Avenue
Washington, D.C. 20501
*http://www.whitehouse.gov/WH/welcome.html*
Through the White House website, you can e-mail the president.

# A Note on Sources

The first thing I did when I started to research this book was to visit Charles Jacobs, president of the Anti-Slavery Society in Massachusetts. He supplied a variety of useful materials. Next, I joined Anti-Slavery International in London, told them my plans, and asked them to send me their frequently published bulletins. I continued my research at my local library where I looked for books on the subject. When I could not find some of the books I needed on the shelves, I ordered them through the Minuteman Library system. With each book I read, I checked their bibliographies to find more sources of information on my topic. I also consulted an atlas of the world to discover where some countries mentioned in my research were located.

I also kept track of current events and discovered many stories about exploited children in daily newspapers and weekly newsmagazines. Even more material came from my computer

# About the Author

**Shirlee Petkin Newman** has written twenty–one books for children, including three for Franklin Watts *Indians* of *the Americas* Series. For Watts Library, she has written *The Pequots*, *The African Slave Trade*, *Slavery in the United States*, and *Child Slavery in Modern Times*. Her other published books include biographies, a picture book, fiction, and folk tales. She has been an Associate Editor of *Child Life Magazine*, published hundreds of stories and articles in other magazines, and has taught writing courses at Brandeis University, Boston Center for Adult Education, and Cambridge Adult Education Center.